Grandma You're the Best!

THIS IS A PRION BOOK

First published in Great Britain in 2016 by Prion
An imprint of the Carlton Publishing Group
20 Mortimer Street
London W1T 3JW

A CIP catalogue for this book is available from the British Library.

ISBN 978-1-85375-952-9

Printed in Dubai

10 9 8 7 6 5 4 3 2 1

Grandma You're the Best!

Humorous and Inspirational Quotes
Celebrating Brilliant Grandmothers

PRION

Contents

Introduction

Grandma, Granny, Nan, Nana, Gammy, Ga-Ga or Gam-Gams – no matter what you call them, it's official, grandmas are the best. They come in all shapes and sizes, and in several disguises, from old and wrinkly to hip and trendy, but one thing is for sure – they are never far away from their gardening tools, crossword puzzles or spectacles, even if they are convinced they are lost!

For many grandkids a trip to granny's house always promises home-cooked meals, being spoilt rotten with ten slices of thick cake, and brand new toys, as well as the guarantee of saying goodbye with pockets of 'spending money'. As a clever wit once wrote, "There is no place like home… except Grandma's." We couldn't agree more. Enjoy!

Grandmas
Rule

"You do not really understand
something unless you can explain it
to your grandmother."

Albert Einstein

"If you would civilize a man, begin
with his grandmother."

Victor Hugo

"A grandmother always has time
for you, even if the rest of the
world is busy."

G. Saunders

"Grandmothers are like snowflakes
– no two are alike."

Janet Lanese

"You have to stay in shape. My grandmother started walking five miles a day when she was 60. She's 97 now and we don't know where the hell she is."

Ellen DeGeneres

"We believed in our grandmother's cooking more fervently than we believed in God."

Jonathan Safran Foer

"As I learned from growing up, you don't mess with your grandmother."

Prince William

"A grandma's name is little less in love than is the doting title of a mother."

William Shakespeare

"My grandmother is over 80 and still doesn't need glasses. Drinks right out of the bottle."

Henry Youngman

"Grandmothers are voices of the past and role models of the present. Grandmothers open the doors to the future."

Helen Ketchum

"A house needs a grandma in it."

Louisa May Alcott

"If God had intended us to follow recipes, he wouldn't have given us grandmothers."

Linda Henley

"Becoming a grandmother is wonderful. One moment you're just a mother. The next you are all-wise and prehistoric."

Pam Brown

"If nothing is going well, call
your grandmother."

Italian proverb

"It is as grandmothers that our
mothers come into the fullness
of their grace."

Christopher Morley

"When a child is born, so are
grandmothers."

Judith Levy

"Just about the time a woman thinks her work is done, she becomes a grandmother."

Edward H. Dreschnack

"If your baby is 'beautiful and perfect, never cries or fusses, sleeps on schedule and burps on demand, an angel all the time,' you're the grandma."

Teresa Bloomingdale

"My grandmother is my angel
on earth."

Catherine Pulsifer

"Grandma always made you feel she
had been waiting to see just you all
day and now the day was complete."

Marcy DeMaree

"Grandchildren don't make a man
feel old; it's the knowledge that he's
married to a grandmother."

G. Norman Collie

"A grandma is warm hugs and sweet memories. She remembers all of your accomplishments and forgets all of your mistakes."

Barbara Cage

"We should all have one person who knows how to bless us despite the evidence. Grandmother was that person to me."

Phyllis Theroux

"If becoming a grandmother
was only a matter of choice, I
should advise every one of you
straightaway to become one. There
is no fun for old people like it!"

Hannah Whithall Smith

"Dear Grandmamma, with what we
give, we humbly pray that you may
live, for many, many happy years:
although you bore us all to tears."

Hilaire Belloc

"Being pretty on the inside means you don't hit your brother and you eat all your peas – that's what my grandma taught me."

Lord Chesterfield

"It's impossible for a grandmother to understand that few people, and maybe none, will find her grandchild as endearing as she does."

Janet Lanese

"When it seems the world can't understand, your grandmother's there to hold your hand."

Joyce K. Allen Logan

"Truth be told, being a grandma is as close as we ever get to perfection. The ultimate warm sticky bun with plump raisins and nuts. Clouds nine, ten, and eleven."

Bryna Nelson Paston

"'You're more trouble than the children are' is the greatest compliment a grandparent can receive."

Gene Perret

"Grandma and Grandpa, tell me a story and snuggle me with your love. When I'm in your arms, the world seems small and we're blessed by the heavens above."

Laura Spiess

"We have become a grandmother."

Margaret Thatcher

"Most grandmas have a touch
of the scallywag."

Helen Thomson

"You are the sun, grandma, you
are the sun in my life."

Kitty Tsui

"Our mothers and grandmothers…
moving to music not yet written."

Alice Walker

"Now that I've reached the age
where I need my children more
than they need me, I really
understand how grand it is to be
a grandmother."

Margaret Whitlam

"Being a grandmother is our last chance to act like a kid without being accused of being in our second childhood."

Janet Lanese

"My grandmother was a very tough woman. She buried three husbands and two of them were just napping."

Rita Rudner

"Changing a diaper is a lot like getting a present from your grandmother – you're not sure what you've got, but you're pretty sure you're not going to like it."

Jeff Foxworthy

"Obviously there was something to this grandmother business. So far as I could tell, it was like being Queen of England, minus the inconvenience of having to wear a crown."

Elizabeth Berg

"A grandmother pretends she doesn't know who you are on Halloween."

Erma Bombeck

"Grandmotherhood initiated me into a world of play, where all things became fresh, alive, and honest again through my grandchildren's eyes. Mostly, it retaught me love."

Sue Monk Kidd

"Grandmother. The true power behind the power."

Lisa Birnbach

"Grandpa Joe: I saw Willy Wonka with my own two eyes. I used to work for him, you know.
Charlie Bucket: You did?
Grandpa Joe: I did.
Grandma Josephine: He did.
Grandpa George: He did.
Grandma Georgina: … I love grapes."

Charlie and the Chocolate Factory

"But Grandmother! What big
ears you have!"

Little Red Riding Hood

"Never balk at being called
'granny'. It's not a dirty word,
even though a friend of mind insists
on being called 'Glammy'.
It's a badge of honour."

Virginia Ironside

"When you get into the granny era,
you're lucky to get anything."

Maggie Smith

"I am where I am today because
my grandmother gave me the
foundation for success."

Oprah Winfrey

"I love being a grandmother. That feeling you have for your own child – you don't ever think it will be replicated, and I did wonder if I would have to 'pretend' with my grandchildren. But my heart was taken on day one."

Joanna Lumley

"I always remember having a healthy respect for my grandmother."

Prince William

"'Grandmother' doesn't mean that you have gray hair and you retire and stay home cooking cakes for your grandchildren."

Carine Roitfeld

"A mother becomes a true grandmother the day she stops noticing the terrible things her children do because she is so enchanted with the wonderful things her grandchildren do."

Lois Wyse

"A lot of the modern action films I see, I just think that any guy could do it. I could take my grandma, put her in a cape, put her on a green screen and do all the action. Anyone can do it."

Jason Statham

"Being a mother and grandmother is the best of the best in my life. My grandchildren multiply the joy my daughters bring me."

Alexandra Stoddard

"Some moments can only be cured
with a big squishy grandma hug."

Dan Pearce

"I spent three weeks pushing a
pan scrubber in the baby's face.
I want him to get used to kissing
his grandmother."

Les Dawson

Young at Heart

"When you're young and beautiful, you're paranoid and miserable."

Helen Mirren

"No spring, nor summer hath such grace. As I have seen in one autumnal face."

John Donne

"The Good Old Days are now."

Tom Clancy

"My grandkids believe I'm the
oldest thing in the world. And after
two or three hours with them,
I believe it, too."

Gene Perret

"To keep the heart unwrinkled,
to be hopeful, kindly, cheerful,
reverent – that is to triumph
over old age."

Thomas Bailey Aldrich

"'Old' is not a dirty word.
Old age is not an illness. It took a
long time and a lot of hard work
to get here and I see no reason to
apologise for my arrival."

Irma Kurtz

"There is a fountain of youth:
it is your mind, your talents, the
creativity you bring to your life and
the lives of the people you love.
When you learn to tap this source,
you will have truly defeated age."

Sophia Loren

"It's not that age brings childhood back again, age merely shows what children we remain."

Johann Wolfgang von Goethe

"Grow old along with me! The best is yet to be, the last of life, for which the first was made. Our times are in his hand who saith, 'A whole I planned, youth shows but half; Trust God: See all, nor be afraid!'"

Robert Browning

"It's not how old you are, it's
how you are old."

Jules Renard

"There is only one cure for
grey hair. It was invented by a
Frenchman. It is called
the guillotine."

P.G. Wodehouse

"Sex at age 90 is like trying to shoot
pool with a rope."

George Burns

"Learning is an ornament in prosperity, a refuge in adversity, and a provision in old age."

Aristotle

"That's the trouble with you young people. You think because you ain't been here long, you know everything. In my life I already forgot more than you ever know."

Neil Gaiman

"When you are old and grey and full of sleep and nodding by the fire, take down this book, and slowly read, and dream of the soft look your eyes had once, and of their shadows deep."

W.B. Yeats

"I'm not senile. If I burn the house down it will be on purpose."

Margaret Atwood

"Old age is not a surprise, we knew it was coming – make the most of it. So you may not be as fast on your feet, and the image in your mirror may be a little disappointing, but if you are still functioning and not in pain, gratitude should be the name of the game."

Betty White

"Cherish all your happy moments: they make a fine cushion for old age."

Christopher Morley

"If I had known I was going to live this long, I would have taken better care of myself."

Mae West

"The good thing about being old is not being young."

Stephen Richards

"Old age is always wakeful; as if,
the longer linked with life, the less
man has to do with aught that
looks like death."

Herman Melville

"You can't help getting older, but
you don't have to get old."

George Burns

"The golden age is before us,
not behind us."

William Shakespeare

"The old believe everything, the
middle-aged suspect everything, the
young know everything."

Oscar Wilde

"Age is an issue of mind over
matter. If you don't mind, it
doesn't matter."

Mark Twain

"Do not go gentle into that good night... Rage, rage against the dying of the light."

Dylan Thomas

"Anyone who stops learning is old, whether at 20 or 80. Anyone who keeps learning stays young. The greatest thing in life is to keep your mind young."

Henry Ford

"Wrinkles should merely indicate
where smiles have been."

Mark Twain

"Age does not protect you from
love. But love, to some extent,
protects you from age."

Anaïs Nin

"Youth is the gift of nature, but
age is a work of art."

Stanislaw Jerzy Lec

"Age appears to be best in four things; old wood best to burn, old wine to drink, old friends to trust, and old authors to read."

Francis Bacon

"Forty is the old age of youth; 50 the youth of old age."

Victor Hugo

"Adults are just outdated children."

Dr. Seuss

"True terror is to wake up one morning and discover that your high school class is running the country."

Kurt Vonnegut

"The great secret that all old people share is that you really haven't changed in 70 or 80 years. Your body changes, but you don't change at all. And that, of course, causes great confusion."

Doris Lessing

"Nature gives you the face you have at 20; it is up to you to merit the face you have at 50."

Coco Chanel

"I don't believe one grows older. I think that what happens early on in life is that at a certain age one stands still and stagnates."

T. S. Eliot

"I'm not interested in age. People who tell me their age are silly. You're as old as you feel."

Henri Frederic Amiel

"You don't stop laughing because you grow older. You grow older because you stop laughing."

Maurice Chevalier

"Age is not important unless you're a cheese."

Helen Hayes

"Old age, believe me, is a good and pleasant thing. It is true you are gently shouldered off the stage, but then you are given such a comfortable front stall as spectator."

Confucius

"Retirement at 65 is ridiculous. When I was 65 I still had pimples."

George Burns

"In youth we run into difficulties.
In old age difficulties run into us."

Beverly Sills

"An archaeologist is the best
husband a woman can have.
The older she gets the more
interested he is in her."

Agatha Christie

"Age is a high price to pay
for maturity."

Tom Stoppard

"I don't feel old. I don't feel
anything till noon. That's when
it's time for my nap."

Bob Hope

"There are two lasting bequests we
can give our children. One is roots.
The other is wings."

Hodding Carter, Jr.

"The really frightening thing about
middle age is the knowledge that
you'll grow out of it."

Doris Day

"Inside every old person is a young person wondering what happened."

Terry Pratchett

"Birthdays are good for you. Statistics show that the people who have the most live the longest."

Larry Lorenzoni

"Growing old is mandatory; growing up is optional."

Chili Davis

"You are only young once, but you can stay immature indefinitely."

Ogden Nash

"There's no pleasure on earth that's worth sacrificing for the sake of an extra five years in the geriatric ward of the Sunset Old People's Home, Weston-Super-Mare."

John Mortimer

"The idea is to die young as late as possible."

Ashley Montagu

"You can live to be a hundred if you give up all things that make you want to live to be a hundred."

Woody Allen

"Life would be infinitely happier if we could only be born at the age of 80 and gradually approach 18."

Mark Twain

"I complain that the years fly
past, but then I look in a mirror
and see that very few of them
actually got past."

Robert Brault

"Age does not diminish the extreme
disappointment of having a scoop
of ice cream fall from the cone."

Jim Fiebig

"Everything slows down with age, except the time it takes cake and ice cream to reach your hips."

John Wagner

"As you get older three things happen. The first is your memory goes, and I can't remember the other two."

Norman Wisdom

"Old age isn't so bad when you consider the alternative."

Maurice Chevalier

"Those who love deeply never
grow old; they may die of old age,
but they die young."

Dorothy Canfield Fisher

"Millions long for immortality
who do not know what to do with
themselves on a rainy
Sunday afternoon."

Susan Ertz

"Don't cry because it is over,
smile because it happened."

Dr. Seuss

"I don't want to achieve immortality
through my work, I want to achieve
it through not dying."

Woody Allen

"The key to successful ageing
is to pay as little attention to
it as possible."

Judith Regan

"What most persons consider
as virtue, after the age of 40 is
simply a loss of energy."

Voltaire

"I'm like old wine. They don't bring me out very often, but I'm well preserved."

Rose Kennedy

"There are three periods in life: youth, middle age, and 'how well you look.'"

Nelson Rockefeller

"My first advice on how not to grow old would be to choose you ancestors carefully."

Bertrand Russell

"As a graduate of the Zsa Zsa Gabor School of Creative Mathematics, I honestly do not know how old I am."

Erma Bombeck

"You are not permitted to kill a woman who has injured you, but nothing forbids you to reflect that she is growing older every minute. You are avenged 1,440 times a day."

Ambrose Bierce

"Old age comes on suddenly, and
not gradually as is thought."

Emily Dickinson

"Old age is no place for sissies."

Bette Davis

"I think your whole life shows in
your face and you should be
proud of that."

Lauren Bacall

"For those of you who don't have grandchildren, get some. Get them on eBay if you have to."

Diahann Carroll

"It is sad to grow old but nice to ripen."

Brigitte Bardot

"We are always the same age inside."

Gertrude Stein

"Whatever poet, orator or sage may say of it, old age is still old age."

Sinclair Lewis

"Let us never know what old age is. Let us know the happiness time brings, not count the years."

Ausonius

"Youth has no age."

Pablo Picasso

"The secret of genius is to carry
the spirit of the child into old age,
which mean never losing
your enthusiasm."

Aldous Huxley

"If you live to be one hundred,
you've got it made. Very few
people die past that age."

George Burns

"If youth knew; if age could."

Sigmund Freud

"The age of a woman doesn't mean
a thing. The best tunes are played
on the oldest fiddles."

Ralph Waldo Emerson

"The secret of staying young is
to live honestly, eat slowly, and lie
about your age."

Lucille Ball

"I don't need you to remind me
of my age. I have a bladder to
do that for me."

Stephen Fry

"Better pass boldly into that other world, in the full glory of some passion, than fade and wither dismally with age."

James Joyce

"Wives are young men's mistresses, companions for middle age and old men's nurses."

Francis Bacon

"At 50, everyone has the face he deserves."

George Orwell

"Setting a good example for your children takes all the fun out of middle age."

William Feather

"Be eccentric now. Don't wait for old age to wear purple."

Regina Brett

"No woman should ever be quite accurate about her age. It looks so calculating."

Oscar Wilde

"Some day you will be old enough
to start reading fairy tales again."

C.S. Lewis

"The older I grow, the more
I distrust the familiar doctrine
that age brings wisdom."

H. L. Mencken

"Just remember, when you're over
the hill, you begin to pick
up speed."

Charles M. Schulz

"One should never trust a woman
who tells one her real age. A woman
who would tell one that would tell
one anything."

Oscar Wilde

"How did it get so late so soon?
It's night before it's afternoon.
December is here before it's June.
My goodness how the time has flew.
How did it get so late so soon?"

Dr. Seuss

"The great thing about getting older
is that you don't lose all the other
ages you've been."

Madeleine L'Engle

"All the world's a stage, and all
the men and women merely
players: they have their exits and
their entrances; and one man in
his time plays many parts, his acts
being seven ages."

William Shakespeare

"I don't believe in ageing. I believe
in forever altering one's aspect
to the sun."

Virginia Woolf

"When people talk about the good
old days, I say to people, 'It's not
the days that are old, it's you that's
old.' I hate the good old days. What
is important is that today is good."

Karl Lagerfeld

"With age comes wisdom, but sometimes age comes alone."

Oscar Wilde

"Hey, even the Mona Lisa is falling apart."

Chuck Palahniuk

"Some men like shiny new toys. Others like the priceless antique."

Donna Lynn Hope

"Too many people, when they get old, think that they have to live by the calendar."

John Glenn

"I have reached an age when, if someone tells me to wear socks, I don't have to."

Albert Einstein

"Do not try to live forever, you will not succeed."

George Bernard Shaw

"By the time you're 80 years old you've learned everything. You only have to remember it."

George Burns

"He who is of a calm and happy nature will hardly feel the pressure of age, but to him who is of an opposite disposition, youth and age are equally a burden."

Plato

"At age 20, we worry about what others think of us. At age 40, we don't care what they think of us. At age 60, we discover they haven't been thinking of us at all."

Ann Landers

"One starts to get young at the age of 60."

Pablo Picasso

"The tragedy of old age is not that
one is old, but that one is young."

Oscar Wilde

"To be 70 years young is sometimes
far more cheerful and hopeful than
to be 40 years old."

Oliver Wendell Holmes, Jr.

"My idea of hell is to be
young again."

Marge Piercy

"Backward, turn backward,
O Time, in your flight, make me a
child again just for tonight!"

Elizabeth Akers Allen

"To get back my youth I would do
anything in the world, except take
exercise, get up early or
be respectable."

Oscar Wilde

Grandkids are the Best

"The reason grandchildren and grandparents get along so well is that they have a common enemy."

Sam Levenson

"Maybe there is no actual place called hell. Maybe hell is just having to listen to our grandparents breathe through their noses when they're eating sandwiches."

Jim Carrey

"Nobody can do for little
children what grandparents do.
Grandparents sort of sprinkle
stardust over the lives of
little children."

Alex Haley

"Uncles and aunts, and cousins,
are all very well, and fathers and
mothers are not to be despised; but
a grandmother, at holiday time,
is worth them all."

Fanny Fern

"The best baby-sitters, of course,
are the baby's grandparents.
You feel completely comfortable
entrusting your baby to them for
long periods, which is why most
grandparents flee to Florida."

Dave Barry

"If I had known how wonderful it
would be to have grandchildren, I'd
have had them first."

Lois Wyse

"Our grandchildren accept us
for ourselves, without rebuke or
effort to change us, as no one in
our entire lives has ever done,
not our parents, siblings, spouses,
friends – and hardly ever our
own grown children."

Ruth Goode

"An hour with your grandchildren
can make you feel young again.
Anything longer than that, and you
start to age quickly."

Gene Perret

"Few things are more delightful
than grandchildren fighting
over your lap."

Doug Larson

"Grandchildren are God's way of
compensating us for growing old."

Mary H. Waldrip

"Grandparents are there to help the
child get into mischief they haven't
thought of yet."

Gene Perret

"I like to do nice things for my grandchildren – like buy them those toys I've always wanted to play with."

Gene Perret

"Surely, two of the most satisfying experiences in life must be those of being a grandchild or a grandparent."

Donald A. Norberg

"What children need most are
the essentials that grandparents
provide in abundance. They give
unconditional love, kindness,
patience, humour, comfort,
lessons in life. And, most
importantly, cookies."

Rudolph Giuliani

"When grandparents enter the door,
discipline flies out the window."

Ogden Nash

"Grandparents, like heroes, are as
necessary to a child's growth
as vitamins."

Joyce Allston

"The secret of life is to skip having
children and go directly
to grandchildren."

Mel Lazarus

"Youth is a wonderful thing. What a
crime to waste it on children."

George Bernard Shaw

"They say genes skip generations.
Maybe that's why grandparents find
their grandchildren so likeable."

Joan McIntosh

"The closest friends I made all
through life have been people who
also grew up close to a loved and
loving grandmother or grandfather."

Margaret Mead

"My great-grandfather used to say to his wife, my great-grandmother, who in turn told her daughter, my grandmother, who repeated it to her daughter, my mother, who used to remind her daughter, my own sister, that to talk well and eloquently was a very great art, but that an equally great one was to know the right moment to stop."

Wolfgang Amadeus Mozart

"The Queen Mother, with a
lifetime's popularity, seemed
incapable of a bad performance
as national grandmother – warm,
smiling, human, understanding,
she embodied everything the public
could want of its grandmother."

John Pearson

"Do you know why grandchildren
are always so full of energy? They
suck it out of their grandparents."

Gene Perret

"Make no mistake about why these babies are here; they are here to replace us."

Jerry Seinfeld

"Children are a great comfort in your old age. And they help you reach it faster, too."

Lionel Kaufman

"Never have children, only grandchildren."

Gore Vidal

"The first half of our lives is ruined
by our parents, and the second half
by our children."

Clarence Darrow

"Grandparents often talk about the
younger generation as if they didn't
have anything to do with it."

Haim Ginott

"I don't want to die an old lady."

Edith Piaf

"No matter how old a mother is, she watches her middle-aged children for signs of improvement."

Florida Scott-Maxwell

"The line between angry young woman and grumpy old lady is very fine."

Judy Horacek

"They told me that grandchildren are the reward you get for not killing your children."

Virginia Ironside

"My mother always used to say: 'The older you get, the better you get, unless you're a banana.'"

Rose, The Golden Girls

"As a daughter, you think you know everything. As a mother you know you know everything. As a grandmother, you know they really don't know diddley."

Jill Milligan

"What I and many grandparents have discovered is that when it comes to advice, less is more. The less you volunteer your opinions, the more you seem to be asked for them."

Gloria Hunniford

Family Comes First

"Family is the most important
thing in the world."

Princess Diana

"My mother-in-law has so many
wrinkles, when she smiles she looks
like a Venetian blind."

Les Dawson

"A baby is born with a need to be
loved – and never outgrows it."

Frank A. Clark

"My advice to you is to get married. If you find a good wife, you'll be happy; if not, you'll become a philosopher."

Socrates

"My husband and I have never considered divorce… murder sometimes, but never divorce."

Joyce Brothers

"Before you marry a person, you should first make them use a computer with slow Internet to see who they really are."

Will Ferrell

"Don't worry that children never listen to you; worry that they are always watching you."

Robert Fulghum

"Few things are more satisfying than
seeing your children have teenagers
of their own."

Doug Larson

"You can learn many things from
children. How much patience you
have, for instance."

Franklin P. Jones

"Let parents bequeath to their children not riches, but the spirit of reverence."

Plato

"Children are our second chance to have a great parent-child relationship."

Laura Schlessinger

"Don't try to make children grow up to be like you, or they may do it."

Russell Baker

"Having children is like having a
bowling alley installed in
your brain."

Martin Mull

"Never raise your hand to
your children – it leaves your
midsection unprotected."

Robert Orben

"My mother protected me from
the world and my father threatened
me with it."

Quentin Crisp

"To show a child what has once delighted you, to find the child's delight added to your own, so that there is now a double delight seen in the glow of trust and affection, this is happiness."

J.B. Priestley

"Holding these babies in my arms makes me realize the miracle my husband and I began."

Betty Ford

"Whether she is a homemaker or career woman, all a grandmother wants is her family's love and respect as a productive individual who has much to contribute."

Janet Lanese

"Two things I dislike about my granddaughter – when she won't take her afternoon nap, and when she won't let me take mine."

Gene Perret

"Have children while your parents are still young enough to take care of them."

Rita Rudner

"It's one of nature's ways that we often feel closer to distant generations than to the generation immediately preceding us."

Igor Stravinsky

"Soon I will be an old, white-haired lady, into whose lap someone places a baby, saying, 'Smile, Grandma!' – I, who myself so recently was photographed on my grandmother's lap."

Liv Ullmann

"Happiness is having a large, loving, caring, close-knit family in another city."

George Burns

"There is no such thing as fun for the whole family."

Jerry Seinfeld

"Rejoice with your family in the beautiful land of life!"

Albert Einstein

"I think it would be interesting if old people got anti-Alzheimer's disease where they slowly began to recover other people's lost memories."

George Carlin

"God could not be everywhere, and
therefore he made mothers."

Rudyard Kipling

"I am sure that if the mothers of
various nations could meet, there
would be no more wars."

E. M. Forster

"All women become like their
mothers. That is their tragedy. No
man does. That's his."

Oscar Wilde

"Mothers are all slightly insane."

J. D. Salinger

"If evolution really works,
how come mothers only have
two hands?"

Milton Berle

"Some of the world's best educators
are grandparents."

Charles W. Shedd

"I phoned my grandparents and my grandfather said 'We saw your movie.' 'Which one?' I said. He shouted 'Betty, what was the name of that movie I didn't like?"

Brad Pitt

"Like all the best families, we have our share of eccentricities, of impetuous and wayward youngsters and of family disagreements."

Queen Elizabeth

"I love music of all kinds,
but there's no greater music
than the sound of my
grandchildren laughing."

Sylvia Earle

"Your sons weren't made to
like you. That's what
grandchildren are for."

Jane Smiley

"Being grandparents sufficiently
removes us from the responsibilities
so that we can be friends."

Allan Frome

"Whenever I see my grandkids
I have an uncontrollable urge to
fling open my arms, excitedly shout
their name and scoop them up."

Jill Davis

"If you live to be a hundred,
I want to live to be a hundred minus
one day, so I never have to live
without you."

A. A. Milne, Winnie the Pooh

"I think in a lot of ways
unconditional love is a myth.
My mom's the only reason I know
it's a real thing."

Conor Oberst

"After a good dinner one can forgive anybody, even one's own relations."

Oscar Wilde

"The homemaker has the ultimate career. All other careers exist for one purpose only – and that is to support the ultimate career."

C.S. Lewis

"Parents are like God because you want to know they're out there, and you want them to think well of you, but you really only call when you need something."

Chuck Palahniuk

"If you cannot get rid of the family skeleton, you may as well make it dance."

George Bernard Shaw

"When your mother asks,
'Do you want a piece of advice?' it's
a mere formality. It doesn't matter
if you answer yes or no. You're
going to get it anyway."

Erma Bombeck

"I have learned that to be with
those I like is enough."

Walt Whitman

"You only live once, but if you do
it right, once is enough."

Mae West

"Live as if you were to die tomorrow. Learn as if you were to live forever."

Mahatma Gandhi

"Imperfection is beauty, madness is genius and it's better to be absolutely ridiculous than absolutely boring."

Marilyn Monroe

"There is nothing like staying at home for real comfort."

Jane Austen

"There are only two ways to live your life. One is as though nothing is a miracle. The other is as though everything is a miracle."

Albert Einstein

"A woman is like a tea bag; you never know how strong it is until it's in hot water."

Eleanor Roosevelt

"A woman's mind is cleaner than a man's: she changes it more often."

Oliver Herford

"Husbands and wives generally understand when opposition will be vain."

Jane Austen

"How can a woman be expected to be happy with a man who insists on treating her as if she were a perfectly normal human being."

Oscar Wilde

"There is no spectacle on
earth more appealing than that
of a beautiful woman in the act of
cooking dinner for someone
she loves."

Tom Wolfe

"The beauty of a woman must be
seen from in her eyes, because that
is the doorway to her heart, the
place where love resides."

Audrey Hepburn

"Back in '68, when I was sweeping up hair in that barbershop, I had this mental picture of the family that, if I was lucky enough, I would end up with. Perfect wife, perfect kids... Well guess what? I didn't get any of that. I wound up with this sorry bunch. And I'm thankful for that every day. Well, most days."

Jay Pritchett, Modern Family

"All happy families are alike; each unhappy family is unhappy in its own way."

Leo Tolstoy

"A mother's love for her child is like nothing else in the world. It knows no awe, no pity, it dares all things and crushes down remorselessly all that stands in its path."

Agatha Christie

"Get a new bra every six months at least and keep it well hitched-up. You don't want to be one of those people whose boobs touch their tummies when they sit down. Or, worse, when they stand up."

Virginia Ironside

"I think baking cookies is equal
to Queen Victoria running an
empire. There's no difference
in how seriously you take the job,
it's how seriously you approach
your whole life."

Martha Stewart

"I may be a senior, but so what?
I'm still hot."

Betty White

"I look back on my life like a good day's work. It was done and I am satisfied with it."

Grandma Moses

"There is nothing nobler or more admirable than when two people who see eye to eye keep house as man and wife, confounding their enemies and delighting their friends."

Homer

Love and
Happiness

"Knitting is very conducive to thought. It is nice to knit a while, put down the needles, write a while, then take up the sock again."

Dorothy Day

"I did this scene in *Lars and the Real Girl* where I was in a room full of old ladies who were knitting, and it was an all-day scene, so they showed me how. It was one of the most relaxing days of my life."

Ryan Gosling

"Happiness is nothing more than good health and a bad memory."

Albert Schweitzer

"I didn't know what Facebook was, and now that I do know what it is, I have to say, it sounds like a huge waste of time."

Betty White

"I have a memory like an elephant. I remember every elephant I've ever met."

Herb Caen

"I have a two-storey house and a bad memory, so I'm up and down those stairs all the time. That's my exercise."

Betty White

"I want a man who's kind and understanding. Is that too much to ask of a millionaire?"

Zsa Zsa Gabor

"The love of gardening is a seed once sown that never dies."

Gertrude Jekyll

"Gardening is learning, learning, learning. That's the fun of it. You're always learning."

Helen Mirren

"Garden as though you will live forever."

William Kent

"When you trip over love, it is easy to get up. But when you fall in love, it is impossible to stand again."

Albert Einstein

"If a thing loves, it is infinite."
William Blake

"To love is nothing. To be loved is something. But to love and be loved, that's everything."
Themis Tolis

"If I know what love is, it is because of you."
Herman Hesse

"Being deeply loved by someone
gives you strength, while loving
someone deeply gives you courage."

Lao Tzu

"The best place to find God is in a
garden. You can dig for him there."

George Bernard Shaw

"We are shaped and fashioned by
those we love."

Johann Wolfgang von Goethe

"Love all, trust a few,
do wrong to none."

William Shakespeare

"Love is that condition in which
the happiness of another person is
essential to your own."

Robert A. Heinlein

"Hugs can do great amounts of
good – especially for children."

Princess Diana

"Always remember that you are absolutely unique. Just like everyone else."

Margaret Mead

"Wine is constant proof that God loves us and loves to see us happy."

Benjamin Franklin

"Laugh and the world laughs with you, snore and you sleep alone."

Anthony Burgess

"Go to heaven for the climate,
hell for the company."

Mark Twain

"When a man who is drinking neat
gin starts talking about his mother
he is past all argument."

C.S. Forester

"A perfect martini should be
made by filling a glass with gin
then waving it in the general
direction of Italy."

Noël Coward

"You know you must be
doing something right if old
people like you."

Dave Chappelle

"There's one more terrifying fact
about old people: I'm going to be
one soon."

P. J. O'Rourke

"Being a mother is an attitude,
not a biological relation."

Robert A. Heinlein

"I exercise strong self-control.
I never drink anything stronger
than gin before breakfast."

W.C. Fields

"Nothing is more responsible
for the good old days than a
bad memory."

Franklin Pierce Adams

"I call the change of life 'orchids' because menopause is such an ugly word. It's got 'men' in it for goddsakes."

Lisa Jey Davis

"Getting older is no problem. You just have to live long enough."

Groucho Marx

"In my house I'm the boss, my wife is just the decision-maker."

Woody Allen

"Since people are going to be living longer and getting older, they'll just have to learn how to be babies longer."

Andy Warhol

"You know you're getting old when the candles cost more than the cake."

Bob Hope

"The great thing about getting older
is that you get a chance to tell the
people in your life who matter what
they mean to you."

Mike Love

"I can honestly say I love
getting older. Then again, I never
put my glasses on before looking
in the mirror."

Cherie Lunghi

"It's a poor sort of memory that
only works backwards."

Lewis Carroll

"As I'm getting older, I'm enjoying
my vices so much more because
I feel like I've deserved them."

Brooke Shields

"But I'm kind of comfortable with
getting older because it's better than
the other option, which is being
dead. So I'll take getting older."

George Clooney

"Male menopause is a lot more
fun than female menopause.
With female menopause you gain
weight and get hot flashes. Male
menopause you get to date young
girls and drive motorcycles."

John Wayne

"Let's face it, a nice creamy
chocolate cake does a lot for a lot of
people; it does for me."

Audrey Hepburn

"All you need is love.
But a little chocolate now
and then doesn't hurt."

Charles M. Schulz

"I'm grateful for every day I'm still
alive. Everything is still working.
I attribute it to eating a lot of
processed foods. I think it's the
preservatives that keep me going.
That, and I eat as much chocolate
as I can get my hands on."

Joan Rivers

"I wish I were a girl again, half savage and hardy, and free... Why am I so changed? I'm sure I should be myself were I once among the heather on those hills."

Emily Brontë

"The advantage of a bad memory is that one enjoys several times the same good things for the first time."

Friedrich Nietzsche

"For beautiful eyes, look for the good in others; for beautiful lips, speak only words of kindness; and for poise, walk with the knowledge that you are never alone."

Audrey Hepburn

"Kindness is the language which the deaf can hear and the blind can see."

Mark Twain

"Whether one believes in a religion or not, and whether one believes in rebirth or not, there isn't anyone who doesn't appreciate kindness and compassion."

Dalai Lama

"You must have been warned against letting the golden hours slip by; but some of them are golden only because we let them slip by."

James M. Barrie

"The heart of a mother is a deep abyss at the bottom of which you will always find forgiveness."

Honore de Balzac

"One of the luckiest things that can happen to you in life is, I think, to have a happy childhood."

Agatha Christie

"You're only given a little spark of madness. You mustn't lose it."

Robin Williams

"Life is full of misery, loneliness, and suffering – and it's all over much too soon."

Woody Allen

"What's the point of children if you can't buy their love?"

Homer Simpson

"I don't plan to grow old gracefully. I plan to have face-lifts until my ears meet."

Rita Rudner

"When you are dissatisfied and would like to go back to youth, think of algebra."

Will Rogers

"I'm at an age when my back goes out more than I do."

Phyllis Diller

"Looking 50 is great... if you're 60."

Joan Rivers

"If I had fantastic legs I might wear short skirts, but I think at 78, one's got to act one's age."

Mary Berry

"The *New York Times* crossword puzzle every morning keeps the old grey matter ticking."

Carol Burnett

"I'm really enjoying my retirement. I get to sleep in every day. I do crossword puzzles and eat cake."

Derek Landy

"There seem to be two main types of people in the world – crosswords and sudokus."

Rebecca McKinsey

"Handmade presents are scary because they reveal that you have too much free time."

Douglas Coupland

"You can't get spoiled if you do your own ironing."

Meryl Streep

"There are 364 days when you might get un-birthday presents, and only one for birthday presents, you know."

Lewis Carroll

"A great marriage is not when the 'perfect couple' comes together. It is when an imperfect couple learns to enjoy their differences."

Dave Meurer

"I didn't marry you because you were perfect. I didn't even marry you because I loved you. I married you because you gave me a promise. That promise made up for your faults. And the promise I gave you made up for mine. Two imperfect people got married and it was the promise that made the marriage. And when our children were growing up, it wasn't a house that protected them; and it wasn't our love that protected them – it was that promise."

Thornton Wilder